To: Clayton/Cyn

He has a plan for you!

Ronn Moyer

COINCIDENCE OR GOD'S PLAN
HEARING GOD'S VOICE

Jeremiah 29:11

BY RONN MOYER

COINCIDENCE OR GOD'S PLAN

Copyright © 2010
by Ronn Moyer
131 Crescent Lane
Harleysville, PA 19438

All rights reserved.

Library of Congress Number: 2010906304
International Standard Book Number: 978-1-60126-234-9

Printed 2010 by
Masthof Press
219 Mill Road
Morgantown, PA 19543-9516

DISCLAIMER

    Since I am not a seasoned writer on theological matters and without special training in related theories and subjects, I recognize my human limitations in the field. I would therefore, appreciate that any reader understands that these are my thoughts and are written in my own words. I believe the Holy Spirit inspired me to write them, but if any person finds fault with the stories or opinions expressed I am hopeful for your understanding. I have been filled with joy as I have come to feel and to realize God working through me—in the past, the present and I believe into the future. I wish the same joy and fulfillment for you.

ACKNOWLEDGEMENTS

Whenever a project such as writing a book comes to consummation there are many people and entities, which contribute to the final product. I was fortunate to have an in-house proofreader who spent some hours reviewing the manuscript, making suggestions and corrections and supporting me with encouragement. Diane, "my favorite wife," allowed me to take over the computer even when Facebook friends called her, so that I could complete writing the book. I appreciate her assistance and friendship.

Leon Moyer shared with me the story of his grandfather and the accident, which caused Elmer to lose his hand and gave permission to use the example of God working through another person.

Craig Smith allowed me to use his descriptions from his recent book entitled *Every Monday*. Craig is District Executive of the Atlantic Northeast District of the Church of the Brethren with oversight to nearly 70 congregations.

I also want to recognize Masthof Press for their many suggestions, support and encouragement during the various book projects in which they have assisted me. Their editing and publishing has been first rate. Their staff has been a pleasure with whom to work.

Most importantly, however, it is necessary for me to acknowledge the leading of the Holy Spirit. When this book was only a thought, I heard the "voice of God telling me to write it." I balked due to my inexperience and lack of self-confidence in writing about theological thoughts and concerns, but was prompted to finish the book because "there would be persons who would benefit from reading it." I pray that the Holy Spirit will be as real to you as He has been to me in working through us all for His glory.

PREFACE

Have you heard God's voice lately? What did it sound like—was it masculine or feminine? Some say, "God speaks through other people." Some say He speaks through nature or through coincidence. Still others say, "God does not speak at all." A few people have shared that God sent an angel and they heard the angel speak. Nearly everyone believes there is a God but it seems that fewer and fewer people believe that they need God on a day-to-day basis. Prosperity and success causes most persons, including professing Christians, to unconsciously believe they are self-sufficient and allow a close relationship with God to wane and die. Why is it so difficult for us to understand and accept the fact that we were created and abide here on earth for *one reason only?* That reason is to praise and bring glory to God our Creator, Lord and Savior. That's why He created us.

Being past seventy years of age I can safely say that I recently had an eye-opener revelation and heard God's voice. That is the reason for writing this book. The experience has frightened me, excited me, inspired me and caused me to be content in allowing His message to flow through me to others. Part of the message I heard was to share my experience with others in the hope that they also will have their eyes opened and become more dynamic Christians. Since I am not a theologically-trained minister, but only an active lay person, I was reluctant to try to put the message into a book. Again I heard the urging of God saying, "Don't worry, I'll tell you what to write" and "I will be with you."

I say, therefore, that this is a message from one layman to another lay person. It is not a book for the clergy to read ☺. It's just between us lay people. Having said that (tongue in cheek), I seriously want to share that I would not want to offend anyone who might take issue with my thinking, beliefs or conclusions. My purpose is not to spank but to encourage readers to pause a moment, back up a bit, and consider how God has been working through you in the past and the present and will in your future days. Let it happen. Encourage it to continue. Now you will be in a position to be much more effective in your witness and association with friends, family and even strangers you meet. The icing on the cake is that you will become more excited about your future with God and your church. Just to realize that God is working through you as an instrument to complete His work here on earth is so special and inspirational.

If anyone is offended by examples or stories I share—because they seem like they are targeting you—please accept my apology. I am not aiming darts at anyone more than at myself. This has been an exciting experience for me and I wish for you to share that excitement as you come to realize your new potential.

CHAPTER 1

I was nearly finished writing my first book for publication. A sense of fulfillment and pride was welling up within me. I often wondered whether or not I could write a book—and if I did, would anyone pay to read it.

The book encompassed much of my life's work and while it was and is interesting to me, it might be boring or seem self-serving to any potential reader. I was required to write fact and to refrain from embellishment in that the project was in large part a history. A book outlining the history of anything must be totally non-fiction; I had to remind myself many times. O, how much fun it would be to allow imagination and storytelling to take over my fingers on the keyboard; but no, I needed to be true to the facts as best as I could recall them and research them. Nevertheless, to me, it felt like a great accomplishment to be nearing a visit to the publisher with whom I had already discussed the printing of the book. I felt proud of my accomplishment and relieved to be completing the final chapter.

Suddenly, like a bolt of lightning, it hit me in the solar plexus. This accomplishment of writing the history of Peter Becker Community along with the various anecdotes and stories of residents, staff and community, was *not my doing*. I had merely been the hands and the mind used by God to make this book happen. No wonder it had been so easy to sit in front of my computer and type story after story and incident after incident for hours at a time. I hadn't typed more than a few letters in the past year prior to that. I have struggled with recollection of names, especially since my sixties. I have been embarrassed with lack of memory retention, and yet these happenings sprang to life, one after another, as fast as I could type them. It seemed as though the story, which covers about 33 years, had just occurred the week or year before and the vision was as clear as could be.

My feelings quickly changed from pride in accomplishment to ones of awe and a bit of fright. I also quickly felt closeness to God as if He were saying, "Ah, you finally begin to get the picture. I have been working through you all your life and only now do you realize what has been happening, and it only took about 60 years!!" Within just a few moments, I realized that not only the book was the product of God's leading but also the whole experience of helping to establish a ministry of service and a home for countless older folks.

It soon became clear that how I got involved in the retirement community was the leading of the Lord. How I had become a manager for a firm in public sales before that with responsibility of hiring, training and managing fourteen men. The pages continued to turn back for me and I realized that the job previous to that involved administrative responsibilities needed in future jobs. Just prior to that job, I had spent two plus years in alternative service in Nigeria, West Africa, teaching in the elementary school, assisting in the administrative offices and teaching some agriculture. Even before that in high school, I felt compelled to select the commercial course and prepare for management in business.

Then a thrill and a new sense of responsibility coursed through me when I was able to look at the entire picture from a small boy to writing the book. Each step of the way was planned and each had a bearing on the next building confidence for what lay ahead. God was directing my decisions and life without my acknowledgement. I hope to show you, the reader, how the same thing may be happening in your life without your awareness.

CHAPTER 2

Many times throughout our lifetimes, we experience events, which happen that surprise us because of timeliness to other events. We have often heard and it is likely we have used the following phrase ourselves, "My, what a coincidence this is or that was." I will be sharing a number of such events and would encourage you to try to determine whether the event was a product of "God's Plan" or merely a coincidence. Some of them may be more clear or certain in your mind than others depending upon your own similar experiences.

I am not suggesting that coincidences never occur and that they are always God's Plan, but I am suggesting that many times it is the voice of the Lord speaking to us through real experiences and we are not realizing it. A close cousin to coincidence is déjà vu, the feeling that something is reoccurring again as it already happened in the past. Or to take a page from Yogi Berra, the great Yankee catcher who said, "It's déjà vu all over again."

What, really, is coincidence? Webster says, "An accidental and remarkable occurrence of events or ideas at the same time, suggesting but lacking a casual relationship."

My hope is that as we revisit some of these "coincidences" you will be able to remember from your own life experience, similar happenings or events. You will be able to feel God working through your own experiences, which took you in the direction you have gone on your life's journey up to this point.

Why are you in your present job or school? Why were you a teacher, builder, plumber, factory worker, trash hauler, or whatever you were during your lifetime to the present? Did someone offer you a job and you took it? Did a deacon ask you to teach a Sunday school class and you did? Did you ask God to lead you in searching for a job or vocation and you believe He did?

Did your dad have a business and you were expected to join him in that work and possibly take over? Have you felt and believed that your choices were a part of God's plan for you?

I would like to share my personal journey and reveal how God has convinced me He was leading, even when I was not aware of it, and even during times I was not being a very good Christian example. My greatest fear in writing about a personal journey is that some who read this might come to believe that I am boasting or bragging about what I did and how I perceive God's hand in it all.

Again, as in past writings, I have felt the hand of God on my shoulder telling me to tell my story. Because it makes me feel vulnerable, I have spent more time procrastinating in writing this book than I should have. Then the thought comes to me as a voice from above, "Don't you believe that I will direct your words so they will reach those who need them?" I object that I am not a learned scholar with degrees in psychology or theology. Again I hear and feel, "Don't be anxious, I am with you." If, then, I truly believe that God has been working through me during my lifetime, then I must not be ashamed to share the story. I pray for humility to do so as a testimony to God and as an encouragement to you.

CHAPTER 3

When I was 10 years old and part of a family and denomination believing in the Anabaptist tradition, I repented of my sins and mistakes, accepted Jesus as my Savior, and was baptized. The method of baptism is not important to the point of this story, but that it happened at that point in my life. Of passing interest may be, that since our roots are with the Church of the Brethren, our belief and custom was and still is to baptize in water deep enough to immerse the entire body and doing so three times forward representing the trinity—in the name of the Father, the Son and the Holy Spirit.

Although far from being mature enough to understand all the expectations and requirements of living a Christian life, I remember clearly, that I was old enough to feel the calling of the Holy Spirit. Whenever preaching occurred and invitation was given to make a decision to receive Christ into my heart, there was a tightness in my chest, which encouraged me to stand and accept the call. I remember asking my parents why I felt this pull inside me and they assured me it was the Spirit urging me to accept Christ as my Savior.

Unfortunately, it took me 60 years from that time to rather suddenly come to the conclusion, that during that entire time, God was leading each important step of the way and was working through me as a conduit to accomplish just a very small part of His will. It is an "awesome feeling," to use a contemporary phrase, when I look back retrospectively and realize "what has been going on" and how this could be happening for so long without my being aware before now. I'm sure Satan did much of the blocking out of what God was doing through me because I now can see how, in so many ways, I could have been more effective in my witness during these years.

It is my goal, through these writings, to try to awaken you, the reader, in the event you have been similarly blinded, to the awesome opportunity that still awaits you whether you are a teenager or a seventy year old or anywhere in between or older. I have come to the conclusion that EVERYONE WHO AT SOME POINT HAS ACCEPTED CHRIST AS THEIR SAVIOR HAS BEEN LIVING OUT HIS OR HER PURPOSE DAY BY DAY IN THEIR LIFE EXPERIENCE WHETHER OR NOT THEY REALIZE IT… EXCEPT those persons who have willfully turned away from God's attempts to direct their lives.

To explain: If during your lifetime, you have definitely felt as though God were calling you to do something such as pastoral ministry, mission work or the like and your reaction has been, "NO WAY LORD, I'm not cut out for that type of work," and you go another direction, then you may not be or have been where God wants you to be. BUT He is still trying to work through you, perhaps in another, smaller way, and would welcome your acknowledgement that you are aware now and wish to know what He wants you to do next with His help.

How does God direct your life, your decisions and your actions? Sometimes through quiet times when we feel His presence and a message occurs to us in our thought process. Sometimes we are inspired by a good book, a challenging sermon, a Sunday school teacher or good music. Following is an example of His speaking through another person.

CHAPTER 4

Some years ago, a good friend of mine at the church, which I attended, was sharing a recent event in his life and I believe, was seeking my reaction. He related to me that he had been teaching an adult Sunday school class for a number of years and that he had just agreed to teach another year. He admitted that he had spent some time considering the challenge before answering in the affirmative, because he was getting up there in years and was not as sharp as he once was. I suggested that he had the option to refuse the invitation to teach another year and that nobody was forcing him to do this. His response was one I shall never forget and it impacted my life and my decision making thereafter. Joe said to me, "Well, I was tempted to refuse the invitation to teach but it occurred to me that the person asking me to accept this responsibility might be a messenger sent by God." He said further, "I know God works through other people to accomplish His tasks and if I said no, I might be saying no to God."

I began to wonder how often I might have said no to God. It may be a good test for all of us to be more careful of what *may be God's call.* Was the visit and challenge by another person to Joe merely a coincidence or was it God's plan? We need to be sensitive to the various ways in which God has and will speak to us. Sometimes it may be through an accident or illness that we come to realize God is speaking, trying to get us to slow down and listen to Him. Sometimes we may simply experience a gift of nature and marvel at its magnificence, beauty and coordination. The preciseness of the intricate flower, the marvel of the wild bird or animal. Nah! No way could a "big bang" by accident have caused all of that to just fall into place. God is still speaking to us through His creations.

Here's another one for you. Consider for a moment, Jesus and the Samaritan woman at Jacob's well.

Jesus, on this particular trip with His disciples decided to travel through Samaria. On many occasions, Jesus and His followers would have skirted Samaria and gone from Judea to Galilee another way. Normally, the disciples would have been with Him, but this time He was alone, resting near the well. Normally, the woman would have come to the well earlier than the sixth hour to avoid the extreme heat of the day in that region, but on this day she came at noon. On most occasions, the woman and Jesus would not have spoken to each other due to schisms existing between Jews and Samaritans—especially a *woman* of Samaria. This time Jesus asks her for a drink of water. Normally, a Samaritan woman would not have been at all receptive to a Jew telling her that He was the Messiah for whom she and her people were looking. This time she hurried to her people and convinced them that this prophet might be the Christ. Result—He stayed two days and many of that town became believers and followers. (John 4:1-42)

    Consider the points of the story. Jesus went through Samaria. He was alone at the well. The woman came at noon when He was there. He asked for a drink. He told her about her life's story. She led her friends and townspeople to Jesus. If this had happened today in our town, what would we say? Each of these happenings was a coincidence. Timing is everything. They just happened to meet. A fortuitous meeting of chance timing. Looking back at this story and knowing who Jesus was and is and will be, we are quick to say, "No, this was not a meeting of coincidence—this was God's Plan. We can feel comfortable in this conclusion because we now have all the facts and know the history. Most of all, we know who Jesus really is and have at least a dim concept of the power and love He represents to us all.

    In your life, how many coincidences can you recall, which when really examined were probably God's Plan being worked out—through you, or through someone else?

CHAPTER 5

"I have been working through you, all your life . . . " The "silent voice" that speaks to us from time to time and causes us to pause and say to ourselves, "Where did that thought or message come from?" We quickly discard it as a wondering mind or something just heard on the radio, TV or iPod. "It took 60 years . . . " the voice continued in my case, and now I was compelled to look back to see when that was. It was shortly after the time I had accepted Jesus as my personal Savior. What were my decisions then? I was approaching the time for high school.

Probably the biggest choice regarding high school in those days was my choice of what curriculum to take—based on where I wished to go or what I hoped to do following graduation from high school. I had three choices—the general course, the commercial course or the academic course. The most difficult, I surmised was the academic since it was basically preparation for entering college after graduation. I quickly discounted this as impossible for me since I was one of six children and my parents were too poor to send children to college. Even working my way through would be impossible because my family would need my working income after high school to support the other children behind me. The general course would emphasize learning the trades and I preferred to think in terms of business management, which was the theme of the commercial course.

At that time and age, this was likely considered a "no-brainer," to use a contemporary phrase. Looking back, however, it must have been God's way of starting me off in learning to run a business, which would come later.

The lyrics of a song say that God uses ordinary people. It would stand to reason that God also trains and teaches ordinary people to do extraordinary tasks.

The training you have received in life may have been elementary, secondary, college or seminary. It well may have been Sunday school. It almost certainly included parents and family and community in concert. Ponder, for a while, what your training was like and what it was intended to serve. Did you train as a nurse, a doctor or a clinician in related fields? Did you train as a welder, mechanic, technician, mason or some other trade or field in which you needed to use your hands in coordination with your mind? Did you train to be a teacher in school or Sunday school, or a minister of the Gospel? Did you train to be a mother? Try to get good training for that or learn on the job and so many have.

Whatever you do or have done, whether trained or "it just comes naturally," you have been allowing God to work through you in some way. Perhaps it is merely saying the right word at the right time. Maybe a favor for a needy person. A compliment to someone depressed. You might have rationalized that you were in the right place at the right time. REALLY? You think your action was merely a coincidence of being there at the right time? I think God plants people at the right place when another needs a lift. Many are the stories of persons preparing to commit suicide, receiving a phone call just in time to change their minds. You may not realize how many times you have been a conduit through which God has and is speaking to others. Perhaps the following story is a bit of an extreme example but it is alleged true and is one to think about.

This experience was alleged to have been written by a hospice physician from Denver. He writes, "I was driving home from a meeting this evening about five o'clock and was stuck in traffic on Colorado Blvd., when the car started to choke and sputter and die. I barely managed to coast into a gas station, glad only that I would not be blocking traffic and would have a somewhat warm place to wait for the tow truck. The engine would not even turn over when I tried to restart it. Before I could make a call for assistance, I saw a woman walking out of the quickie mart building. It looked like she slipped on ice and fell into a gas pump dropping some of her groceries. I got out of my car to see if she was all right.

"When I got to her side, it looked more as though she had been overcome by sobs than that she had fallen. She was a young woman who looked really haggard with dark circles under her eyes. She dropped something else as I was helping her to get up so I picked it up and gave it to her—it was a nickel.

"At that moment, everything came into focus for me: the crying woman, the ancient suburban vehicle crammed with three kids in back (one in a car seat), and the gas pump reading $4.95. I asked her if she was OK and if she needed help and she just kept saying, 'I don't want my kids to see my crying!' We stood on the other side of the pump from her car for a while until she composed herself. She said she was driving to California and that things were very hard for her right now. So I asked, 'And you were praying right?' That made her back away from me a little, but I assured her I was not a crazy person and said, 'He heard you, and He sent me.'

"I took out my credit card and swiped it through the card reader on the gas pump so she could fill up her car completely. While it was fueling, I walked to the McDonalds next door and bought 2 big bags of food, some gift certificates for more, and a big cup of coffee. She gave the food to the kids in the car, who attacked it like wolves. We stood by the pump eating fries and talking a little bit.

"She told me her name and that she lived in Kansas City. Her boyfriend left two months ago and she had not been able to make ends meet. She knew she wouldn't have money to pay rent come January 1, and finally, in desperation, had called her parents, with whom she had not spoken in five years. They lived in California and said she could come live with them and try to get on her feet there.

"She packed up everything she owned in the car and told the kids they were going to California for Christmas, but not that they were going to live there. I gave her my gloves, a little hug and said a quick prayer with her for safety on the road. As I was walking over to my car, she said, 'So, are you like an angel or something?'

"This definitely made me cry. I said, 'Sweetie, at this time of the year the angels are really busy, so sometimes God uses regular people.' It was so incredible to be a part of someone else's miracle. And of course, you guessed it, when I got in my car it started right up and got me home with no problem. I'll put it in the shop tomorrow to check, but I suspect the mechanic won't find anything wrong. Sometimes the angels fly close enough to you that you can hear the flutter of their wings." One big coincidence? I think not!!! God's Plan being worked out through people like you.

CHAPTER 6

"I have been working through you all your life . . ."

After high school, if you are convinced you cannot go to college due to your home and family situation, the natural thought processes cause questions to arise. What do I do now? What do I want to become of myself? At seventeen years plus, few really know what they want to be or become. The one clear certainty is that I must find a job to support myself and help support my siblings. I was also aware that just around the corner, conscription or "the draft" awaited my compulsory decision. The thought of being required to perform either military service or alternative service for two years or more felt like a huge roadblock just ahead after receiving the freedom experienced by completing high school. The reality of seeking employment of a meaningful or permanent nature was foreign to any plan viewing the prospect of needing to begin all over again after service.

During high school I had acquired part-time work at a nearby hardware store, which I enjoyed very much. I was pleased, therefore, that my employer accepted me on a full-time basis after graduation. This answered my concern of having good employment up until my requirement from the draft board would be fulfilled. I never thought of that work as preparatory for future life, but retrospectively, I believe God was planning my training for future work. It afforded me a wonderful opportunity to meet all kinds of people. It taught me to help people with problems—electrical, construction, plumbing, and mechanical—and how to fix things. While some of these skills were hereditary, the job I had helped me polish those skills as I learned all about tools, paints, parts, nuts, bolts, screws and all those goodies you find in hardware stores. Customers began to ask for me knowing I could "help" them with product and skills. It also taught me how to react and work through customer complaints and to control my emotions.

I now ask the question, "Was this practical training and education by experience, a part of a large coincidence, or was it part of God's Plan working through me?" I can see such a comfortable evolvement of decisions and events pointing ahead that today I have no question that it was God's Plan. Back then, I did not even consider God had any part in these decisions and I would probably have scoffed at anyone suggesting it.

While pondering the relationship of seeing God's Plan in everyday tasks and work I was reminded of an article I read about a physician recognizing God's hand in human physiology and creation. He heard a DVD sermon by Louie Giglio and was amazed by the Apostle Paul's writing correlating with today's medical terms. Louie was talking about how inconceivably BIG our God is and how He spoke the universe into being and how God also knitted our human bodies together with amazing detail and wonder. At this point, the physician said, he was very interested and fascinated from a medical standpoint. He shares how during medical school he learned more and more about God's handiwork and theorized how ANYONE could deny that a Creator had to have done all this.

Suddenly, Giglio began talking about laminin and the doctor says he almost lost his breath. He knew about laminin from medical school. Laminins are a family of proteins that are an integral part of the structural foundation of membranes in almost every animal tissue. Literally laminins are cell adhesion molecules which hold us together. They hold one cell to the next and without them we humans would literally fall apart. While the doctor knew this from book knowledge he was intrigued by application to Christian principles. His further research, for the first time, showed him what laminin looks like. He was now really engrossed and involved since the pictures in medical journals and other scientific and medical pieces of literature show that the image of the laminin is a perfectly shaped cross. (You can google laminins and see the chemical picture of this substance and how it forms a perfect cross as well as a retelling of this story.)

He mused that the glue that holds us together—all of us—is in the shape of the cross. Rev.

Giglio then referenced Colossians 1:15-17 where the Apostle Paul wrote some 2000 years ago before the discovery or naming of laminins was even a thought. "FOR BY HIM ALL THINGS WERE CREATED; THINGS IN HEAVEN AND ON EARTH, VISIBLE AND INVISIBLE, WHETHER THRONES OR POWERS OR RULERS OR AUTHORITIES; ALL THINGS WERE CREATED BY HIM AND FOR HIM. HE IS BEFORE ALL THINGS, AND IN HIM ALL THINGS *HOLD TOGETHER.*"

Contemporary thought and knowledge now evidence that from a very literal standpoint, we are held together . . . one cell to another . . . by the cross. The physician writing this says, "You would never in a quadrillion years convince me that this is anything other than the mark of the Creator who knew EXACTLY what laminin 'glue' would look like long before Adam even breathed his first breath."

We could say and believe that we are being held together by the cross of Jesus Christ. By His love, His forgiveness and His marvelous power.

We could theorize that Paul's inspired words, "He created us and in Him all things hold together," and the discovery of laminins today, which fit this scripture as though an answer to Paul, was one large coincidence. Personally, I cannot buy that. I believe it is all part of God's Plan for us.

CHAPTER 7

"I have been working through you, all of your life . . ."

As I approached my eighteenth birthday, I experienced a certain amount of angst regarding the law of conscription, as it would apply to me. I realized for some years that I was a pacifist and strongly believed that going into active military service was against my religious beliefs. I felt some relief in knowing that our government had recognized that there would be men who were conscientious objectors based on religious beliefs. I was also aware that I would need to prove to an unsympathetic draft board that my feelings were legitimate and well based. I would also be subjected to peers and veterans who would see my stance as avoidance or spurious in nature.

Having been born and raised in the denomination of the Church of the Brethren, it was a bit easier to get a sympathetic ear from the draft board. During those years, our denomination, along with the Quakers and Mennonites were seen and judged as "peace churches" or denominations. It was still soul searching and worrisome to literally stand in front of four questioners in a convincing fashion and finally be granted a 1-O classification. This meant I was physically fit for service and was allowed to exercise my right to serve in alternative service of some kind. Through all of this, I certainly did feel the support of and guidance of the Holy Spirit. In looking back, I am convinced that I believed in salvation through Jesus, but probably thought too little of the Spirit's leading except at times of acute need. Almost like a band-aid is handy when a cut happens.

I was grateful to receive the 1-O classification and it meant that I had a certain period of time to a deadline when I would be required to enter approved alternative service. In the back of my mind, I had this recurring thought that if I received my 1-O classification I would apply to the Brethren Volunteer Service (BVS) program. Back then it was a thought, now I realize it was the leading of God's Spirit. I enrolled and was accepted to a learning/training unit to convene at New Windsor, Maryland, in March of '55.

We had 18 members in the training unit of which 6 were gals and 12 guys. Training was required to strengthen our witness and determine our skills and abilities so that we could be assigned tasks and projects corresponding to out gifts and talents. After two months of half-day study and half-day clothing processing for needy families around the world, we were apprised of the projects, which were actively looking for supply from our BVS unit. Incidentally, during our two months training while the rest of our unit was involved in sorting and baling clothing to go abroad, I was asked to work in the central offices due to having shorthand, typing and commercial training. Again, a different path opened for me and I attributed it to my skills instead of realizing it was another one of God's Plans for me, which would be important in the balance of my career.

I was hoping to be assigned to a foreign project mostly for the travel and adventure aspect, but I was informed early on that usually those projects were assigned to college grad students. Since I had only completed high school at that point, I responded by choosing as my first choice, a volunteer assignment in Puerto Rico. I judged that even though it was off U.S. soil it was not too "foreign" and might be acceptable. I was elated to be selected for a position at Castener Hospital in Puerto Rico and immediately began to study Spanish in my spare time. After our unit evaluation held at Camp Swatara, and about the time arrangements were being made for passports and visas, for those needing them, I was approached by one of our unit leaders and informed that the project in Puerto Rico had been closed and I would not be going there. I was asked if I would consider a spot on the mission field in Nigeria, West Africa.

I was pleasantly surprised to be offered this opportunity, but I didn't realize it was God working through me. I had been singled out to do office work during training and now was asked to accept a position in the Executive Field Offices of our mission in Garkida, Nigeria. Coincidence??

Doors were opening that I didn't recognize. It was so easy back then as a nineteen-year-old guy, to assume that my own smarts, looks and maturity were designing an adventure of the grandest scale. I was confident that I could do this! Yes!!

Time would be needed to prepare for this journey. I would need to have about five inoculations and soon begin taking oral medication for the prevention of malaria, which was prevalent in Nigeria. Clothing needed to be purchased and I was able to get my parents involved in that process. A new passport and various visas needed to be applied for and waiting for that process was causing impatience on my part.

During the interim of waiting, some of us going on foreign projects were assigned to the National Institutes of Health in Bethesda, Maryland, to be used as normal control patients. (Some folks referred to us as guinea pigs.) I was assigned to the fourth floor at this huge medical center, which was the "mental health floor." We were almost immediately introduced to testing for causes and cures for schizophrenics of which there were a couple patients on that floor.

During the ensuing weeks I was tested using lysergic acid, better known as LSD. That was prior to the emergence of LSD on the illicit drug scene. But, that's a whole other story. One aspect of this experience that I have not yet figured out is why they assigned me to the mental floor while all the other BVSers were assigned elsewhere. Perhaps they were trying to tell me something.

The main point of writing this book is to encourage you the reader to think back over your life so far and realize how God has led you in whatever you have been doing. It is also important to experience how it feels to have the Spirit using you as a conduit to carry the work and ministry of God to others.

I shall refrain from getting into detail regarding our journey to Nigeria and the adventure and experiences there since that was already recorded in another book I had the pleasure of writing. That book is entitled *Swimming with Crocodiles* and speaks specifically of the two plus years I spent there. In this book we want to examine coincidences and God's Plan for each of us.

Allow me to share a true story, which happened as I was a boy growing up and which turned out to be a real eye opener to our congregation. During that period of the 1950s and 60s we had as many as six ministers/preachers at the same time. That was called the free ministry when none of these men were paid by the congregation but needed to be employed outside the church to feed their family. These men were called by a system of faith and prayer to do this work and usually none of them had training or schooling as a minister of the Gospel. Most of these ministers pursued special training after they were voted into the ministry. These ministers took turns in the pulpit from one Sunday to the next and shared visitation responsibilities.

Some years later, after these men became older or passed from the scene, the congregation installed a paid pastor who did nearly all the preaching. Anyway, I digress a bit. One of the six ministers, by the name of Elmer Moyer (not related to me), was a farmer by vocation. Near the end of the summer season, he and his son Paul were harvesting the field corn and using it to fill their silo. During that procedure, the corn stalks got stuck in the crusher/blower machine, which shoots the ensilage to the top of the silo. Elmer cut the power so he could unclog the corn stalks as he had done before, but did not realize that the turbine was still winding down and had not yet stopped. As he reached into the chute to pull out the corn stalks stuck there, the blades chopped and mangled his hand. They would soon learn that the mangled hand would need to be amputated.

Leon Moyer, a grandson of Elmer, was a Boy Scout and later a Boy Scout leader. The night before this accident, Paul was perusing Leon's Boy Scout manual and came across the guidelines for needing and applying a tourniquet in order to staunch excess bleeding in an accident producing a severe incision. As it happened, when they extracted Elmer's arm and hand from the silo filler machine, he was bleeding profusely. Paul immediately wrapped his farmer's hanky around Elmer's arm and with a corn cob he fashioned a tourniquet, winding it tightly until they reached the hospital

The doctor in the emergency room inquired about the tourniquet and informed the family that Elmer would certainly have expired had it not been for Paul's handiwork. Think about it for a while and answer the obvious question. Was the happenstance of reading about tourniquets the previous night and the life-saving action by Elmer's son an uncanny coincidence or was it God's Plan. I recall many years beyond that terrible accident, seeing Rev. Elmer raise his black-sock covered stump into the air for emphasis during his sermons. He influenced many of us young teens for good and was a favorite preacher. God was working through all three—Elmer, Paul and Leon—without a doubt.

CHAPTER 8

"I have been working through you, all your life . . ."

Why did I end up in a place like Garkida, West Africa? I didn't ask for this project, it was not even one of my first three listed. The unit director came to me and said, "The project in Puerto Rico has closed and we would like you to consider going to the Church of the Brethren Mission Field in Nigeria." I did not hesitate to say yes but my reaction was because I was looking for adventure, for travel, for seeing the world . . .

God, on the other hand, was speaking to the final decision maker in the matter and most likely saying to Ivan, our director, "Challenge Ronn to go. I have loaned him skills, which can be useful in Nigeria and am preparing him for humanitarian work in the future. He wants adventure, I'll give him both adventure and also make him sensitive to the needs of the people in Nigeria so that he will be more compassionate and useful to me later in his life." God's way of getting my attention and training me for future "mission" work was to place me in a setting of disease, danger, lack of nearly all conveniences and absolutely no social life for a young unmarried man. It was a difficult two years in many ways but in looking back, I can say it was also two of the most meaningful years of my life.

After the novelty of the place and people wore off, those of us in BVS over there began counting the days until we could return—to the conveniences, the automobiles, the TVs, the dating opportunities and the sports. When, finally, we were on our way home to the States, after our projects were completed, we found that we were bringing with us a new compassion for those needing and hurting in our own country. We had developed both a conscious and unconscious yearning and need to help others in some way. How could we do this and prosper at the same time? Again, as I look back, I can see how God's Plan was unfolding in spite of my ignorance of His plan.

Wake up and be aware that God is the pilot, even when you think and believe you are. You have a purpose! "And we know that in all things God works for the good of those who love Him, who have been called according to His purpose." (Rom. 8:28) Even if you have not considered *your purpose* in life recently or even if you have not considered that you are walking in God's Plan each day, consider that He is trying to guide you and lead you and waiting for your cooperation. Believe me, it is an unparalleled relief and positive experience to feel this and realize it. Think how much more effective you can be going forward from this day knowing that God is working through you for His purposes.

Does that scare you? It will encourage and enthuse you as you allow it to penetrate your conscious self and realize that someone so big as our God would even know you exist. But it is true. Just pray to God and say, "OK, if You are out there and working through me or if You want to do this and if I have not been cooperative, then show me how I can do this better. Work through me and use me to be a testimony to those around me including my family."

You may say, "But I'm only a stay at home mother and housewife." Don't ever say ONLY A MOTHER. That may be the most important function of a Christian—to allow God to teach your children and family through you. That's where it all begins. You will encourage your child to listen for God's voice, to learn of His love for us, to take the child to Sunday school and church so the child can be learning about God as you are strengthened through the fellowship of other concerned parents looking to do the right thing.

You may see yourself as only a carpenter, a farmer, a truck driver or bus driver, a cabinetmaker, a mechanic, a painter, a plumber, an auctioneer, a refuse hauler, a toll taker or whatever—the list goes on and on. The fact is, God needs you to function wherever you are in your life, even if retired. No matter what you do you encounter people. What kind of example have you been in how you talk, your body language, the stories you tell? Is profanity ever on your lips? Are you sometimes drinking too much or leering at the opposite sex while you are married? Are you overly enamored with things like that flat screen or iPod or deluxe cell phone or super texter and upgrades on the computer? We need to show others that we are different when it comes to how we deal and communicate with people. What do we do with "Love one another" and "You shall have no other Gods before me?" Are the vehicles we drive practical or intended to tell others how successful we think we are? Are all of our toys becoming our gods?

Purpose!! "We have been called according to His purpose." These promises are just as valid today as when they were written. And they are valid for you whatever you are facing today, and what is yet to come in 2010 and beyond. Renowned Bible teacher Alan Redpath wrote, "There is no circumstance, no trouble, no testing, that can touch me until, first of all, it has gone past God and past Christ, right through to me. If it has come that far, it has come with a great purpose, which I may not understand at the moment. But I refuse to become panicky, as I lift up my eyes to Him and accept it as coming from the throne of God for some great purpose of blessing to my own heart."

Purpose!! We were each created and live for the *purpose* of bringing praise and glory to our God and Creator. How well are we carrying out our purpose? Our loving God is trying to work through each of us. Let it happen!!

CHAPTER 9

"I have been working through you all your life . . ."

This became the period of my life when I became more materialistic and probably walked further away from God. Some reasons why this happened are now obvious to me but back then I would have argued otherwise. It was a time when I had completed the obligation to my country to perform service of some kind. It was coming home to many distractions, which were new and enticing. I was twenty-two years old and had less than $500 in the bank. I needed a job. I was excited about all the eligible young females who were available and hoped to date a few. I had applied for college entrance and was accepted, but alas, I could not pay tuition and buy a car and have any social life unless I got a "good job making good money." My past employer had promised me, that a job would be waiting for me after service and I was grateful for that. It would at least be a job and produce meager income until I could find a better situation.

For an employer to hold open any job for 2 $\frac{1}{2}$ years is noteworthy and I was truly lucky to have work immediately. I was not as grateful as I should have been, taking the rehire too much for granted and being dissatisfied with the salary. I began looking around and within a year another new company offered me a position, which would pay nearly twice as much. I jumped at the opportunity and six weeks later was informed by the owner that he could not make it financially and was going out of business. I was given one-week notice. I had purchased a reasonably good used vehicle through a loan with the bank and could not be without income. Now I could not be choosy nor could I spend a lot of time researching the market.

I asked around about job opportunities and someone pointed me to a company that was growing quickly and hiring. The company was a snack food, retail, door-to-door business. Immediately, I was reminded that when I was a boy of twelve to fourteen, I regularly assisted my dad on his retail baker route when I was not in school, such as during the summers and on Saturdays. It was the kind of work I knew I could do and had confidence when approaching the manager seeking a job opportunity. It happened that they had an opening immediately due to opening a new territory. It also happened that the company seemed excited about my former experience in retail sales and in the confidence I exuded.

Was the fact that there was an immediate opening (I did not lose 1 day of work between jobs) and that it was a job with which I was familiar AND a salary plus commission pay system—a coincidence—a lucky break? You could call it that. I on the other hand remember it as a turning point in vocational life where God was pointing me in a certain direction. It was an opportunity to be reimbursed proportionate to the degree of work and effort I put into it. I could make my routes as large as I wanted by knocking on doors in my territory and the more I made for the company, the more I got paid. It was causing me to learn to meet all kinds of people, to develop relationships through honesty and dependability of service. It was like running my own business. Where was it pointing me? I did not recognize the opportunity as a plan of God then but it was easy to see it and feel it years later.

At the time of my hiring, there were already twelve men employed servicing routes one through twelve. I became route thirteen and was not superstitious of the number. I remember that it was the autumn of the year and that by the next year as we were entering the Christmas season, I was finally near capacity with customers, which I could handle in a two-week rotation service. We had ten separate routes—five one week and five the next so that we served our customers once every two weeks. During the busy Christmas season when we also featured homemade chocolates and Christmas candies, I was fortunate to be the first driver in the short history of the company to sell more than $1,000.00 worth of product in one week.

Shortly after the holidays, I was promoted to regional manager of the operation and assigned the counties of Lehigh and Northampton in east central

Pennsylvania. It became my job to solicit new customers, open new routes and territories, hire men to run the routes, and handle the finances of the branch operation. I was given a new vehicle every two years for my personal use as well as all my driving to and from the Allentown, Bethlehem and Easton areas.

It was during this time that I married my sweetheart and we began our family. Diane was a lifetime member of the Indian Creek Church of the Brethren as I was and we still are. Both our fathers were ordained ministers in the denomination. We fashioned an apartment on the farmstead where Diane was born and spent the next ten years living there having one daughter and one son two years apart. It was a time of making good money, driving new vehicles, taking vacations and starting our family. It was also a time to have Satan convince me that I was pretty self sufficient and capable of making my own life's decisions.

We always attended our church faithfully and still do, but Diane was more the spiritual head of our family which I realized only years later. During the tenure of my work in retail sales, which lasted 12 years, I was able to grow the regional company from three part-time routes when I began, into 13 full-time routes. I was responsible and able to hire men for each of these routes and was also assigned a supervisor to assist me and run any of the routes when required.

I was fortunate to have a kind and supportive employer who was co-owner of the companies, the one I managed and another in the Bucks and Montgomery County area. It was customary for my employer to hand me an envelope near Christmas with the comment, "This is for you outside the salary and payroll system. I want you to enjoy Christmas and not to pay taxes on this gift." There was usually $500 cash in the envelope and back in the early 1960s, that was an extremely generous gift. That same year, our congregation was beginning a fund raising effort to establish a retirement community in the town close by and since we were prospering well otherwise, we passed the $500 gift on to the committee. We theorized that someday our parents might need such a place and we would like it to be close to home. I don't think we ever envisioned it being a future home for ourselves.

CHAPTER 10

"I have been working through you, all your life . . . "

Only a few weeks after making that end-of-year contribution to the committee planning a new retirement community, I received a phone call from one of the committee. I was not surprised since I expected either a letter of receipt or a call thanking us for the gift. After expressing their thanks, the committee person informed me that I was nominated to the ballot of the annual meeting of this new non-profit corporation as a potential member of their Board of Directors, and would I be willing to serve if elected?

This question surprised me and caused me some instant concern. First, I had no particular interest in assisting in the planning for a new retirement community and second, I was really becoming busy growing the business in Allentown and we were expecting our first child. Many days, including travel time, I spent twelve hours working and driving. I inquired as to how my name had come up as a potential board member and was informed that the contribution we had made entitled both Diane and me to become members of the corporation. The Board of fifteen members, both male and female, were attempting to get a representative number of "younger" board members to balance the mostly "retired age" members already on the board.

I recall that during this conversation, I had some feelings of "this might be interesting" and "I should be doing something church related and helpful to others." The caller was convinced that due to my business background as well as service time in Africa, I would have talent to offer the new board. I finally answered that so long as there were not too many meetings and so long as the meetings were in the evening, I would accept the challenge to at least allow my name on the ballot. I never thought of this as a call from God or a part of His Plan for me until years later when I was inspired to review my life journey and it became so obvious.

Consider the course of happenings in a short span of time. My boss decided to hand me a $500 cash gift. For some reason, Diane and I agreed to pass the gift along to the committee working on a new retirement community. Unbeknownst to us, the gift was an automatic qualifier for corporate membership to this new corporation. Because our names appeared on a membership list of those qualified to serve on the Board of Directors, I was nominated to that position. I was subsequently voted onto the board and a committee to do detail planning for the newly-envisioned ministry to older folks in the community.

This may have all been coincidence!?! I look back and both see and feel the hand of God on my shoulder, leading me into that ministry. It also felt right. It felt like my experiences of teaching and helping families and older folks in Nigeria was a platform from which I could assist in a project of true altruism.

At least, I felt eager to explore just how I might make a difference in this new idea for our community.

If we are open to the opportunities around us, God will find us and in some way, challenge us to allow Him to work through us to help others. I'm reminded of a true story I recently read in my email, another possible coincidence but I think part of God's Plan and "grist" for this book.

Rev. John Powell is a professor at Loyola University in Chicago. He tells the story of a student he encountered and how the student finally challenged Professor Powell to spread his story to others. I'll do my part to assist by retelling his story.

"Some twelve years ago, I stood watching my university students file into the classroom for our first session in the Theology of Faith. That was the day I first saw Tommy. My eyes and my mind both blinked. He was combing his long flaxen hair, which hung six inches below his shoulders. It was the first time I had ever seen a boy with hair that long. I guess it was just coming into fashion then. I know in my mind that it isn't what's on your head but what's in it that counts; but on that day I was unprepared and my emotions flipped. I immediately filed Tommy under 'S' for strange . . . very strange.

"Tommy turned out to be the 'atheist in residence' in my Theology of Faith course. He constantly objected to, smirked at, or whined about the possibility of an unconditionally loving Father/God. We lived with each other in relative peace for one semester, although I admit he was for me at times a serious pain in the back pew.

"When he came up at the end of the course to turn in his final exam, he asked in a cynical tone, 'Do you think I'll ever find God?' I decided, instantly, on a little shock therapy. 'No!' I said very emphatically. 'Why not,' he responded, 'I thought that was the product you were pushing.' I let him get five steps from the classroom door and then I called out, 'Tommy! I don't think you'll ever find Him, but I am absolutely certain that He will find you!' He shrugged a little and left my class and my life. I felt slightly disappointed at the thought that he had missed my clever line—He will find you! At least I thought it was clever. Later I heard that Tommy had graduated, and I was duly grateful.

"Then a sad report came. I heard that Tommy had terminal cancer. Before I could search him out, he came to see me. When he walked into my office, his body was very badly wasted and the long hair had all fallen out as a result of chemotherapy. But his eyes were bright and his voice was firm, for the first time, I believe. 'Tommy, I've thought about you so often; I hear you are sick,' I blurted out. 'Oh, yes, very sick. I have cancer in both lungs. It's a matter of weeks . . . ' 'Can you talk about it Tom?' I asked. 'Sure, what would you like to know?' he replied. 'What's it like to be only twenty-four and dying?' 'Well, it could be worse.' 'Like what?' I quickly responded.

"'Well, like being fifty and having no values or ideals, like being fifty and thinking that booze, seducing women, and making money are the real biggies in life.' I began to look through my mental file cabinet under 'S' where I had filed Tommy as strange. (It seems as though everybody I try to reject by classification, God sends back into my life to educate me.) 'But what I really came to see you about,' Tom said, 'is something you said to me on the last day of class.' (He remembered!!) He continued, 'I asked you if you thought I would ever find God and you said, 'No!' which surprised me. Then you said, 'But He will find you . . .' I thought about that a lot, even though my search for God was hardly intense at that time.' (My clever line—he thought about that a lot.)

"'But when the doctors removed a lump from my groin and told me that it was malignant, that's when I got serious about locating God. And when the malignancy spread into my vital organs, I really began banging bloody fists against the bronze doors of heaven. But God did not come out. In fact, nothing happened. Did you ever try anything for a long time with great effort and with no success? You get psychologically glutted, fed up with trying. And then you quit.

"'Well, one day I woke up, and instead of throwing a few more futile appeals over that high brick wall to a God who may be or may not be there, I just quit. I decided that I didn't really care about God, about an afterlife, or anything like that. I decided to spend what time I had left doing something more profitable. I thought about you and your class and I remembered something else you had said. 'The essential sadness is to go through life without loving. But it would be almost equally sad to go through life and leave this world without ever telling those you loved that you had loved them.

"'So, I began with the hardest one, my Dad. He was reading the newspaper when I approached him. 'Dad.' 'Yes, what?' he asked without lowering the newspaper. 'Dad, I would like to talk with you.' 'Well, talk.' 'I mean, it's really important.' The newspaper came down three slow inches. 'What is it?' 'Dad, I love you, I just wanted you to know that.' Tom smiled at me and said it with obvious satisfaction, as though he felt a warm and secret joy flowing inside of him. The newspaper fluttered to the floor. Then my father did two things I could never remember him ever doing before. He cried and he hugged me. We talked all night, even though he had to go to work the next morning. It felt so good to be close to my father, to see his tears, to feel his hug, to hear him say that he loved me. It was easier with my mother and little brother. They cried with me too, and we hugged each other and started saying real nice things to each other. We shared the things we had been keeping secret for so many years.

"'I was only sorry about one thing—that I had waited so long. Here I was, just beginning to open up to all the people I had actually been close to.

"'Then, one day I turned around and God was there. He didn't come to me when I pleaded with Him. I guess I was like an animal trainer holding a hoop, 'C'mon, jump through. C'mon, I'll give you three days, three weeks.' Apparently God does things in His own way and at His own hour. But the important thing is that He was there! You were right. He found me even after I stopped looking for Him.'

"'Tommy,' I practically gasped, 'I think you are saying something very important and much more universal than you realize. To me, at least, you are saying that the surest way to find God is not to make Him a private possession, a problem solver, or an instant consolation in time of need, but rather by opening to love. You know the Apostle John said that. He said, 'God is love and anyone who lives in love is living with God and God is living in him?' Tom, could I ask you a favor? You know, when I had you in class you were a real pain. But (laughingly) you can make it all up to me now. Would you come into my present Theology of Faith course and tell them what you have just told me? If I told them the same thing, it would not be half as effective as if you were to tell it.' 'Oooh, I was ready for you, but I don't know if I'm ready for your class.' 'Tom, think about it. If and when you are ready, give me a call.'

"A few days later, Tom called, said he was ready for the class; that he wanted to do that for God and for me. So we scheduled a date. However, he never made it. He had another appointment, far more important than the one with my class and me. Of course, his life was not really ended by his death, only changed. He made the great step from faith into vision. He found a life far more beautiful than the eye of man has ever seen or the ear of man has ever heard or the mind of man has ever imagined. Before he died, we talked one last time. 'I'm not going to make it to your class,' he said. 'I know, Tom.' 'Will you tell them for me? Will you . . . tell the whole world for me?' 'I will, Tom. I'll tell them. I'll do my best.'

"So, to all of you who have been kind enough to read this simple story about God's love, thank you for listening. And to you, Tommy, somewhere in the sunlit, verdant hills of heaven—I told them, Tommy, as best I could."

God was working through Tommy, but it took a tragedy and premature death by cancer for Tommy to share his story. His story affects lives in a positive way, even after his demise. God continues to work through Tommy's story even today.

CHAPTER 11

"I have been working through you, all your life . . ."

As the weeks and months passed, I became more and more involved and interested in working with the Board of Directors planning the new retirement home for older church and community people. I was quite busy with my sales management position and with travel, which consumed sixty or more hours per week. Therefore, as things progressed with the plans for beginning the new retirement community, I found myself too busy. Both of these time-consuming endeavors were interesting and important to me and I tried to give them whatever effort I could.

Many times, years later, I bemoaned the fact that during those years, I relinquished much of my responsibility as a father and husband to "important work and planning." My wife, Diane, became both mother and father by default on many occasions. It is one of my life's greatest regrets, that I didn't spend more time with my daughter and son during their formative years. There is no going back and correcting that, it is just one piece of advice I can pass on to my children and friends. It is something for which I solicit my family's forgiveness. Spend time with your children while they are in your care because too soon they are grown and on their own.

As we progressed with the planning of the retirement community, we decided on a name and incorporated as a non-profit corporation. A piece of ground was located on the edge of Harleysville, twenty acres in size, and the Board decided to begin raising funds, along with the auxiliary which had formed, to purchase the land. The twenty acres abutted an important historical site of the denomination. (Another coincidence, or was it God's Plan?) The first bishop of the Church of the Brethren to move from Germany to this country is buried in the cemetery on this historical spot. Also, erected years later in 1843, a small country church building still stands next to the cemetery and is on the national registry of historic sites. That bishop's name was Peter Becker and the church is the Klein Meeting House. The name of the corporation we formed was Peter Becker Memorial Home, which later became and is today, Peter Becker Community.

Both the Board of Directors and the Auxiliary were working hard and became more and more involved time wise. We all felt dependant on the Lord for guidance since none of us had intimate knowledge of how to plan, build, or run such an operation. We spent many hours in prayer and definitely felt the movement of the Holy Spirit in the day-to-day planning. I viewed my position as one where I was helping these "older members" to accomplish their goal. I was asked to accept the position of Vice President of the Board in the early 1960s and with overwhelming feelings of inadequacy agreed to take on added responsibility. I still did not view this as a personal life's path or work, just another job to work through. If someone had asked me, during those days, if I believed that God was working through me to accomplish a goal, I probably would have said, "No, I'm just doing volunteer outreach for our church and the older members."

We sometimes, unconsciously, come to believe and assume that things are working out in our work or in our lives because we are intelligent or smart and because we work hard. We need to understand that our very intelligence and ability to work at anything, are gifts loaned to us from God. He has allowed us to be successful, whatever that is, to see what we will do with that success. He has allowed us to be financially stable to see how we will use our wealth. He is working through us each day to see how loving we will be to our neighbor—to see how we will support those in need around us—to see if we are sharing our testimony as we have opportunity. If we are prohibiting His work from flowing through us, we are working against His will. This makes Satan happy. We need to be awake to God's presence within us on a daily basis. I say again; the main reason we were put here on earth is to "praise God, from whom all blessings flow."

God loves you and He is working through you. He forgives all past mistakcs and sins if we sincerely repent and ask Him. How effective God's work through you is, is directly related to your recognition of that fact and your cooperation as a channel through whom His love and message can work. What an awesome feeling when we realize this and it is first frightening, then inspiring as we encourage the Holy Spirit to direct us each day.

CHAPTER 12

More and more time was required in the planning processes than I had bargained for. Our Board was beginning to learn how much is involved in such a venture as creating and beginning a new retirement community. The first parcel of ground was purchased and some of the Board members gave and loaned their own money to make it happen. An architect was selected and engaged after interviewing five or six potential firms. Rough drawings were created as we corporately shared our dreams of what we each thought would be needed. As we neared final decision time, there was some degree of anxiety on behalf of the Board and conversation regarding whether or not we could really pull this off. We considered that we might be dreaming and having visions, which would end up being more than we could handle or afford.

We needed to begin with a facility large enough to exercise efficiencies of staff time and supply purchases, but small enough to be able to handle the up front costs without experiencing business failure right from the start. The architect's estimate of initial building costs for a first phase, including all costs and furnishings slightly exceeded one million dollars. For 1970 dollars, this seemed like an unreachable goal. Some felt we should scrap the whole idea and give back funds already raised. We prayed about this and felt lead by the Lord to forge ahead carefully.

It was about this time, for some unknown reason, I made a comment to the effect that, "If this facility ever does get built, I would have some interest in administration if the Board would be agreeable to hiring me." I felt that based on my business management experiences it would be an interesting and challenging opportunity. Looking back, I believe a couple men on the Board were praying that I would become involved in a direct way. They challenged me, at that same board meeting, to consider beginning immediately as Director of Development and Fund Raising, to work at raising the funds, which would be needed to begin construction with the carrot that I would be welcome to become administrator as we looked to begin operations.

I'm sure I reacted with both shock and disbelief as I responded, "Yeah, right, what do I know about raising funds?" We had interviewed a couple firms of "professional fund raisers," but were reluctant to pay their high fees feeling that too many of the dollars raised would go back into the pockets of the fund raisers. I was floored to learn that the Board was very serious in their asking and I responded, "I have a good job and good salary, two small children and a wife at home who need to be considered and with whom I would need to discuss such a possibility."

We were also looking to build our first home and I needed to consider closely, the financial concerns this might present. It was interesting to be an officer of the Board and to know that we probably "couldn't afford me" unless I took a severe cut in wages. We had nearly completed payment for the 20 acres, which cost us $30K and we were looking at raising a million. How did I ever get into this position? I guess I should have kept my mouth closed. I needed time to ponder the ramifications. First order of business was to approach my wife with such a proposal and solicit her wisdom.

Was it just a coincidence that I happened to be on the Board of Peter Becker Community? We often talk about being at the wrong place at the wrong time. Is the reverse true—being at the right place at the right time? I am reminded of a true story of a lady who went into a Starbucks in New York to warm up one day, told through the eyes of a musician who was playing there at the time. She calls it "The song that silenced the cappuccino machine . . ." It was chilly in Manhattan but warm inside the Starbucks shop on 51st Street and Broadway, just a skip up from Times Square. Early November weather in New York City holds only the slightest hint of the bitter chill of late December and January, but it's enough to send the masses crowding indoors to vie for available space and warmth. For a musician, it's the most lucrative Starbucks location in the world, I'm told, and consequently, the tips can be substantial if you play your tunes right.

Apparently, we were striking all the right chords that night, because our basket was almost overflowing. It was a fun, low-pressure gig—I was playing keyboard and singing backup for my friend who also added rhythm with an arsenal of percussion instruments. We mostly did pop songs from the '40s to the '90s with a few original tunes thrown in. During our emotional rendition of the classic, "If You Don't Know Me by Now," I noticed a lady sitting in one of the lounge chairs across from me. She was swaying to the beat and singing along.

After the tune was over, she approached me. "I apologize for singing along on that song. Did it bother you?" she asked. "No," I replied. "We love it when the audience joins in. Would you like to sing up front on the next selection?" To my delight, she accepted my invitation. "You choose," I said. "What are you in the mood to sing?" "Well . . . do you know any hymns?" "Hymns?" This woman didn't know who she was dealing with. I cut my teeth on hymns. Before I was even born, I was going to church. I gave our guest singer a knowing look. "Name one." "Oh, I don't know. There are so many good ones. You pick one." "Okay," I replied, "how about 'His Eye is on the Sparrow?'" My new friend was silent, her eyes averted. Then she fixed her eyes on mine again and said, "Yeah, let's do that one."

She slowly nodded her head, put down her purse, straightened her jacket and faced the center of the shop. With my two-bar setup, she began to sing, "Why should I be discouraged? Why should the shadows come?" The audience of coffee drinkers was transfixed. Even the gurgling noises of the cappuccino machine ceased as the employees stopped what they were doing to listen. The song rose to its conclusion. "I sing because I'm happy; I sing because I'm free. For His eye is on the sparrow, and I know He watches me." When the last note was sung, the applause crescendoed to a deafening roar that would have rivaled a sold-out crowd at Carnegie Hall. Embarrassed, the woman tried to shout over the din, "Oh, y'all go back to your coffee! I didn't come in here to do a concert! I just came in here to get somethin' to drink, just like you!" But the ovation continued. I embraced my new friend. "You, my dear, have made my whole year! That was beautiful!" "Well, it's funny that you picked that particular hymn," she said.

"Why is that?" "Well . . ." she hesitated again, "that was my daughter's favorite song." "Really!" I exclaimed. "Yes," she said, and then grabbed my hands. By this time, the applause had subsided and it was business as usual. "She was 16. She died of a brain tumor last week." I said the first thing that found its way through my stunned silence. "Are you going to be okay?" She smiled through tear-filled eyes and squeezed my hands. "I'm gonna be okay. I've just got to keep trusting the Lord and singing His songs, and everything's gonna be just fine." She picked up her bag, gave me her card, and then she was gone.

Was it JUST A COINCIDENCE that we happened to be singing in that particular coffee shop on that particular November night? Was it coincidence that this wonderful lady just happened to walk into that particular shop? Was it coincidence that of all the hymns to choose from, I just happened to choose the very hymn that was the favorite of her daughter, who had died just the week before? I refuse to believe it. God has been arranging encounters in human history since the beginning of time, and it's no stretch for me to imagine that He could reach into a coffee shop in

RONN MOYER

Midtown Manhattan and turn an ordinary gig into a revival. It was a great reminder that if we keep trusting Him and singing His songs, everything's gonna be okay. The next time you feel like GOD can't use YOU, just remember . . .

Noah was a drunk; Abraham was too old; Isaac was a daydreamer; Jacob was a liar; Leah was ugly; Joseph was abused; Moses had a stuttering problem; Gideon was afraid; Sampson had long hair and was a womanizer; Rahab was a prostitute; Jeremiah and Timothy were too young; David had an affair and was a murderer; Elijah was suicidal; Isaiah preached naked; Jonah ran from God; Naomi was a widow; Job went bankrupt; John the Baptist ate bugs; Peter denied Christ; the Disciples fell asleep while praying; Martha worried about everything; the Samaritan woman was divorced, more than once; Zaccheus was too small; Paul was too religious; Timothy had an ulcer; AND Lazarus was dead! No more excuses now!! God can use you to your full potential. Besides, you aren't the message, you are just the messenger.

CHAPTER 13

"I have been working through you, all your life . . ."

Looking back from today's vantage point, it was a decision, which did not make logical sense. It was a risk with a young family, to consider changing jobs for a twenty percent cut in salary. Diane supported my decision either way and showed confidence in whatever I decided. I must have been motivated by challenges back then and accepted the proposal of the Board to begin full-time employment as Director of Development and Fund Raising. I remember some "down on my knees time" about that time, asking the Lord to "lead me to the people who had money and would support our dream," because I frankly did not know where to begin.

As the weeks went by, pledges, contributions and loans were made at a much more accelerated pace than we could have hoped for. The community was ready for such a facility and the timing was good. I WAS BEING LED BY THE LORD to green pastures, and yet, unconsciously, gave daily credit to myself for my talent in finding donors and supporters and convincing them to part with their money for a project which had no guarantee of success. There was no equity beyond the 20-acre piece of ground we had bought, which was now about paid off.

The Board decided to purchase a dated Plymouth sedan for me to use to get around, since I no longer had a new company car to drive every two years. Perhaps they were not too sure I would last as long as the car they bought for me. The outcome of this adventure in faith was successful enough for us to break ground one year after I began and produced enough cash to complete the first phase and open for business two plus years later with space for 72 residents.

I will not use more than modest reference to particulars in the complicated process of beginning such an endeavor, but to say that it was much more complicated than any of that original Board of Directors ever envisioned. In the book entitled, *I Want to Go Home* which I mentioned before, I wrote in the preface the following truism, "A Board without knowledge of how to start or run a retirement/nursing facility; a fund raiser with no experience in raising funds, an original staff with no experience in operating a retirement/nursing facility and an Administrator who had never done this work before—to have seen an idea move to a ministry serving nearly 500 residents in program, facilities and care today is a MIRACLE. To *God be the glory, great things He has done.*

So, we see exhibited, both hope and faith. A small group of believers had a hope that such a Continuing Care Retirement Community could happen in their community. They had faith that if they prayed and believed their prayers would be answered in a positive and tangible way. In Hebrews 6:18-19 we read, "We who have fled to take hold of hope offered to us may be greatly encouraged. We have this hope as an anchor for the soul, firm and secure."

Over 350 years ago, one Jeremy Taylor wrote a simple faith statement embracing both hope and faith and can still be a focus for all of us: "Faith is the Christian's foundation, hope is his anchor, death is his harbor, Christ is his pilot, and heaven is his country."

During the beginning years of the ministry at Peter Becker Community, I took a great deal of pride in helping to create a ministry that would have a good reputation. We stressed the use of the phrase, "Christian Ministry" and determined to develop policy based on Christian principles. I think I emphasized this because it was expected. It could not hurt. It was good publicity. It would encourage support. It would attract good quality staff and residents. I prayed for daily guidance and was basically satisfied that things were going well because of the excellent plant we had built and furnished and the excellent employees who helped to get things started. However, as in so many of life's situations, when things are going good, we unconsciously determine that we need less divine help. When problems arise, we can fall back on prayer, our pipeline to God to help us get out of the mess. When that works, our evaluation of the experience is that we were successful in using the tools available to us for that particular problem.

I did not recognize that God was working through me on a day-to-day basis and pointing me in the directions I needed to go. I felt like I was the pilot and God was my co-pilot. He was my spare tire, in case of a flat. I now realize that all along, God was the pilot and I was co-pilot. He was the driver and I was merely a passenger. While I thought I was clever and wise and exercising judgments and decisions, which worked out, it was a product of self-sufficiency and personal skills. Frankly, I was very, very fortunate that my Lord stuck with me until I learned that *no ability or action on my part was anything more than the direct hand of God working through the wisdom and intelligence, which He had loaned me in the first place.* I was merely a tool in His vast toolbox. Praise be to God for His patience and love for all of us.

How much of your life is the direct result of answered prayer and God's working through you without ever being aware it was happening? Let's give God the glory, for it belongs to Him. To us, much has been given—of us, much will be required. What an exhilarating experience to realize we are channels through which God works daily. What an awesome opportunity to be more effective in our Christian walk if we realize this, accept it, encourage it and use it for His glory!!

CHAPTER 14

I've learned over the years that God speaks to us in so many ways but as busy Christians, we often do not slow down enough or become quiet long enough to hear. Just as I heard a "silent voice" when it said, "I have been working through you, all your life . . . ," there have been many times in both my life and yours when thought processes run messages through our heads and we respond to them somewhat casually and unconsciously, without considering why the thoughts came to us. Indeed, it may have been God's voice using us as a conduit through which He can minister. But, we must be very careful because it could also be Satan's voice urging us to do his biding.

You saw a racy or risqué picture on a magazine while passing through the bookstore and considered buying it to see what was inside. You decided a large flat screen was needed, even though the budget would not permit such an expensive luxury. God gave us wisdom and the ability to discern so that we would hopefully follow the right thoughts and voices. This way, it would be our decision and not make us robots of His will.

Even in our churches, Satan has a way of confusing us when we try to make corporate decisions. We need to train ourselves to recognize God's voice. Craig H. Smith is the District Executive of the Atlantic Northeast District of the Church of the Brethren in Pennsylvania, having oversight of nearly 70 congregations. In his recently authored book, *Every Monday*, he writes, "While much of the institutional church wrangles over budgets, flowers, building projects, choir seating, carpet color, padding on pews, staff employment, sermon length, pastoral imperfections, worship styles or music preferences, Jesus still *calls His people by name and waits to see if they will recognize His voice.* He continues to defy death and show up in unexpected places. He stands among us and waits to see if anyone will notice."

During my term as Administrator at Peter Becker Community, I prayed each day for guidance and often had thoughts flash through my head. The thoughts I assumed to be my own brain's telling me what to do and how to do it. I needed to make good decisions and often make them quickly without time to consider ramifications. Still I did not understand or give credit to God answering my prayers but accepted the thoughts that came to me as a product of my own wisdom and ability.

I recall working on the annual budget for operations. My practice would be to come back to the office about 7 or 8 in the evening, lock myself in my office and work on the budget, usually completing it by seven o'clock the next morning. Working through the night with no knocks on my door and no phone ringing allowed concentration to the task. From 1973 through 1980, this was my *modus operandi* and during those years it was all longhand. We had no computers and all the work was by pencil and calculator. Both the Board and I were pleased that those budgets all came within

2% or less of actual operational experience. Still, I believed that the Lord was looking over our operations as a Christian ministry but felt that I alone had done the work of planning, calculating and running the operations. But now I can more clearly see that again, it was God working through me to accomplish His Plan. Do you recognize God's voice?

I have become intrigued with coincidence, as you have learned by now in reading this book. While I was typing this chapter, my computer signaled that I had incoming messages. I took a break to see who left a message and one of the messages was from a Pastor/Chaplain friend in the Lancaster, Pa., area who has a ministry of sending out daily messages of encouragement. His message today was about using the Bible as our guide, listening for God's message and not to be entrapped by worldly fascinations and gadgets, which divert our attention away from following His will. He ended with the following prayer.

"Father, your warnings regarding the deluge of deceitful tactics from the enemy is evidenced all around us—through the media, books, false prophets and even well-meaning but confused individuals. Your Word is the stabilizing and authoritative doctrinal manual for all that I need for life and godliness. You promise to bring maturity into my Christian walk as I apply your teaching so that I attain to the fullness of your son, Jesus Christ, the chief cornerstone. Help me to be wise, studied and vigilant so that I correctly discern good from bad and truth from error. In your holy name I pray, Amen."

How about that; he was sending the same message, "discerning good from bad, truth from error" listening for God's voice, not the devil's. What a coincidence to have the same two messages meet at my desk. Coincidence? Really? Or God's Plan?

CHAPTER 15

Consider Abram/Abraham in the Old Testament. Abram and his wife Sarai are disappointed that they could not produce any children. Sarai convinces Abram to sleep with her maidservant Hagar so that a child could be born to their household. It happens and the boy is named Ishmael. Two wives in the same household produce friction like almost always happens, and Hagar runs off with Ishmael. Hagar runs out of water in the desert and begins crying. She leaves Ishmael a stone's throw away under a bush so that she does not need to watch him die. The Angel of the Lord appears and sends Hagar back to Sarai to make up. Abram is 87 years old when Ishmael is born. Time goes by and the Lord makes a covenant with Abram—changing his name from Abram to Abraham.

The Lord further tells Abraham that he will be a father of a massive nation whose descendants will number with the stars of the sky and the sands of the seashore. Abraham chuckles a bit and offers the fact that Sarah (who has been renamed as the "Mother of many nations") is already 90, considered too old to bear children. Abraham is also 99 years of age and is wondering how this would be possible. After all, they haven't been able to have children all their lives and the Lord tells Abraham that Ishmael is not to be the "Father of many nations" successor to him. I suppose Abraham was thinking, boy, it is about time we get started if this thing is going to happen!!

The Lord further tells Abraham that within the year a son will be born to Sarah and he is to be named Isaac. This also happened and some years later, while Isaac was still a young boy, the Lord decided to test Abraham regarding his faithfulness and his fear of God. He appeared to Abraham and told him to take his son to a place three day's walk away and to sacrifice him as a burnt offering on one of the mountains near

COINCIDENCE OR GOD'S PLAN

Moriah. Can you imagine? After all this time having an only child, being promised that a great nation of thousands of descendants will follow, and now getting a message from God to sacrifice your only son? WAIT a minute, I'm now around 110 years old and something is wrong with this picture. Hey Lord, is my hearing going bad? Would you mind repeating that last directive? I love Isaac and he is my only son.

The scriptures, however, record that Abraham had no question or response of hesitancy. He prepared wood for the sacrifice took a flame in his lantern, told two servants to prepare for a hike, had Isaac get a good night's rest and set out in the morning in the direction of Moriah, awaiting further direction as he went. All Isaac and the servants knew was that they were going to an appointed place, yet to be named by God to make a sacrifice. This child must have asked a hundred times, "Are we there yet?" Three day's walk is rather tiring for a 110 year old and also for a young boy, who likely used up lots of energy along the way tossing stones, running after critters, etc., etc.

They finally arrive at a spot, which was recognized by Abraham, through the leading of the Lord, and stopped there. Abraham instructs the servants to wait here for us and we will be back soon. He takes the fire and the knife and loads some wood on the back of Isaac and off they go. They took only a few steps when, I suspect that Isaac says, "STOP for a minute! We've got the fire, the knife and the wood but where is the lamb to be sacrificed?" Abraham, almost nonchalantly seems to say, "Not to worry, God will provide the sacrifice." They climb to the summit of the hill and there Abraham and Isaac drop their materials and begin to fashion an altar with stones, readily available on the hilltop.

Can you imagine Isaac being quiet all during this altar preparation? I can't. He must have been pestering Abraham repeatedly with such talk as, "Hold it a minute Dad; why are we plaguing ourselves with this work and we forgot an animal for the sacrifice?" But Abraham, being human, must have said to himself, "Lord, we're getting pretty close here and you know I don't really want to sacrifice Isaac. No disrespect intended of course." I would think that the building of the altar took longer than it might have, giving the Lord time to effect an answer to Abraham's dilemma.

Not according to scripture. We read and feel urgency in Abraham to fulfill God's commands.

Now he is finished building the altar so he takes the rope he brought along and begins to tie the arms and legs of Isaac preliminary to placing him on the altar. Can you envision the reaction of any normal boy 10 to 12 years old? "Hey, wait just a minute, old man, are you going crazy or what? You're not getting me on that altar; I like living too much for this game." We don't read about any struggle. If there was one, it must not have been too severe because we next picture Isaac trussed and laying on the altar.

Abraham doesn't stop and look up and say to God, "You're really serious about this aren't you?" No, it is recorded, that Abraham forthwith took the knife and raised it up preparatory to plunging it into the heart of Isaac, his only beloved son, when a sharp voice said, "ABRAHAM! ABRAHAM! Do not lay a hand on the boy! Do not do anything to him. Now I know that you fear God because you have not withheld from me your son, your only son." Do you recognize this story in relationship to the sacrifice of Jesus on the Cross many years later? Abraham showed the allegiance to God that he needed in order to fulfill God's promise to supply multitudes of descendants to Abraham's progeny. God showed His love to us by allowing His one and Only Son to be sacrificed so that we could experience eternal life.

Abraham looked up and there in the thicket, caught by its horns, was a ram. He took the ram and offered it on the altar in place of Isaac. Isaac must have decided then and there not to take any more treks with his aging dad. What a relief for both Isaac and also for Abraham, but what a marvelous and strong faith exhibited by Abraham. WOW! Was the ram in the thicket a wonderful coincidence? You might say it was a miracle. I'll agree to that. The ram would have perished if caught in the thicket for more than a day or two, so it is easy to believe that a miracle of God caused it to be there when needed. But it was not a coincidence, it was all part of God's Plan.

CHAPTER 16

"I have been working through you, all your life . . ."

The ministry at PBC grew and expanded much more quickly than anticipated. As this happened, more and more excellent and dedicated employees applied for employment and were hired to work with our team. It would be natural to ask, "Who sent these employees?" I am sure it had little to do with attraction to already hired staff or myself. These new employees were moved by the Holy Spirit to join us as a result of our prayers to send good people to help us. How do I know this? There were just too many excellent, caring applicants who instantly became a part of the family to believe that it just happened by chance or coincidence. They may not know they were divinely sent, but I believe I know they were.

Funds to assist in our consideration of expansion continued to arrive even long after active solicitation had ceased. Administration and Board were amazed at the responses of the people in the community and churches around us. God was working through all of us even while many of us were not realizing it. Plans for significant expansion were made just two years after opening the original facility. Volunteerism and functions of the Auxiliary more than kept pace with growing operations. Indeed, these unpaid supporters became a necessary support and encouragement to total operations and a force important to success.

Two disappointments are recalled as I think back and consider God's Plan and His leading in my life during these times. I desired, from the outset of establishment of the program, to see a "beautiful Chapel" erected at the apex of our campus. I felt it would be a sign to the public and to residents living here, that we intended to be a Christ-centered ministry to aging persons. The other biggie on my personal wish list was an aquatics program including a beautiful swimming pool. It would bring better health through water exercise and an attraction to choosing PBC as a retirement home. The Lord, however, showed me the meaning of the word patience.

Disappointment on both these projects stemmed from the fact that the residents already living on campus turned thumbs down on these ideas. I was surprised and a bit upset that I could not entice support from them. The crux of the matter was money. The residents, as a group, were convinced that if we completed either of these projects, their monthly rates would skyrocket. They seemed content to worship in the all-purpose room and convince themselves that a good aquatics program was not worth a possible increase in rates. We all seem to encounter times, mostly through impatience, when we wonder WHY? I remember being disappointed and asking WHY. An example of being patient and waiting on God's Plan came to me as I read a short story about a teenage girl who complained to her mother, "Why me mom? What did I do to deserve this?"

As she was complaining to her mother, the mother was baking a cake. Her mother responds, "Would you like a piece of my cake?" The daughter responds, "Absolutely Mom, I love your cake." "Here, have some cooking oil," her mother offers. "Yuck!" says her daughter. "How about a couple raw eggs?" "Gross, Mom!" "Would you like some flour then, or perhaps some baking soda?" "Mom, those are all yucky!" To which the mother replies, "Yes, all those things seem bad all by themselves, but when they are put together in the right way, they make a wonderfully delicious cake!"

God works the same way. Many times we wonder why He would let us go through such bad and difficult times. But God knows that when He puts these things all in His order, they always work for good! We just have to trust Him and eventually, they will all make something wonderful! God is crazy about you. He sends flowers every spring and a sunrise every morning. Whenever you want to talk, He'll listen. He is present anywhere in the universe, and He also chose to live in your heart.

The Chapel materialized nearly 20 years after operations began. It is located exactly where I envisioned it should be, on the corner of our Campus Center with a thirty-foot high cut glass window facing west. It is more versatile and beautiful than I envisioned. The therapy and exercise pool arrived a few years later when the local YMCA agreed to build a new facility on our property, open to all our residents and staff as well as the public. Now we not only have the pool, but also wellness areas with weight and exercise equipment, a gymnasium for walking or games and a whole multitude of classes and opportunities more than we could ever have imagined. If we had built a Chapel or a pool when I wanted them, they would have been obsolete shortly thereafter due to size and capacity requirements now needed. Who said, "Good things come to them that wait?" When God put the plan together, it was the right time and size.

CHAPTER 17

Somewhere or sometime during these years of Administration, it occurred to me that I should retire while operations and finances are going well and positive. For some reason, 25 years seemed like a good goal if health allowed. It being a high-pressure type position, I had seen a significant number of colleagues either retire early or even pass from the scene through heart attack or sickness. After nearly 23 years as C.E.O., I was diagnosed with prostate cancer. Since it was contained to the gland, I opted to have radical surgery and remove the prostate gland. It seemed like therein was a message from God confirming I needed to be serious about retiring. Although I was able to bounce back quickly from the surgery, I set a date at the end of 1993 when I planned to retire, giving the Board a year and a half notice of my intentions and time to procure a replacement.

During these later years, especially as my intended retirement was announced and became known, many staff, Board and family members made comments to me that since I was one of the last original Board, I should write a history about the beginnings to the present. Many times, in social gatherings I was reminded of crazy stories about the comments and actions of residents—especially as they became slightly confused and lost their inhibitions. In relating such stories, I was always careful to avoid using real names so as to protect the dignity of the person involved. Invariably, however, someone would say to me, "Ronn, you should write a book." After hearing the comment scores of times from a variety of people, I pondered the prospect. I had never written much although I did enjoy writing articles or speeches I sometimes gave.

Writing, however, took a back burner when I gave serious consideration to retirement. I was one of many who viewed retirement as something huge in scope and a benchmark in life anticipated throughout my adult life. Now I could sleep in every morning, do whatever I wanted to each day, travel a bit and really enjoy life. One gets the feeling of "I deserve it. I worked hard for many years."

And so, at the conclusion of 1993, I handed the reins over to our Assistant Administrator, Rod Mason, and cleared out my office and went home. I was asked to remain on the Board after retirement but refused because I long have been an advocate for cutting the ties in those kinds of situations and leaving the responsibilities in another's hands. To stay in the administrative mix would be to continue to be looked to and consulted for future guidance over the head of the next administrator. I feel this is good policy for pastors as well as continuing care retirement community administrators. Leave when things are going well and all is in order and cut the ties cleanly. I remained available to the new administration to be called, but promised I would not interfere with their authority in future years.

During the first week of retirement I received a call from an old friend with whom I grew up and with whom I formerly socialized prior to marriage. During our high school days we both played football and even sang in the same quartet infrequently. Merrill at that time was President of a local bank and trust company. I remember Merrill's conversation that day. He said, "Ronn, I have a job in which I think you might be interested." My response was, "Merrill, I just retired last week and I didn't know I was looking for a job." In truth, I *was* hoping to find something part time as a bridge to total retirement. The bank was interested in my becoming a Trust Officer to work with aging persons in the development of their estate planning.

My challenge was to open offices within the various dozen or so continuing care retirement communities within a twenty-mile radius. I would contact my former colleagues in these facilities and propose a service to assist their residents with drafting wills, powers of attorney, living trusts, marital exclusion trusts and documents of those types. Merrill knew that I had gained a good bit of experience as an administrator because of working with our own residents and their various financial and legal questions and requirements over the years.

I was not only interested but excited since this was basically an extension of the type of work I had been doing, but I could set my own hours and days and to some degree establish my own rate of remuneration. Accepting this challenge, showed me a very definite need when I learned from many of these residents that they did not have updated documents they really needed such as living wills and powers of attorney which they more and more were required to have to live in retirement facilities.

I share the forgoing detail to again share how God's Plan, in my case, was continued even after retirement. The former positions and responsibilities I experienced in former employment and schooling played directly into this new experience. I had learned to work directly and confidentially with older persons. I had knowledge of the various products the bank and their attorneys used and required in estate planning and most important, to me at least, was opportunity to share with these "new customers" how they could be better stewards of their wealth.

Many of my contacts had never considered supporting charitable entities through their wills and trusts. They needed advice on how to remember their churches, colleges, retirement communities and other worthwhile charities. It was gratifying to find that most of them did include these beneficiaries when counseled regarding their spiritual responsibilities to giving and the tax implications inherent therein. It was gratifying to me to feel good about helping others and also helping their favorite charitable interests.

This new experience for me, again felt like the Lord was working through me to accomplish the Lord's work. It was a way to assist the future financial needs of churches, colleges and retirement communities and other worthy charities while at the same time causing the resident making the decisions to feel good about their own generosity and unselfishness. In that respect, we were also able to help the Lord work through other persons as well.

CHAPTER 18

"I have been working through you, all your life . . ."

My claim throughout this book is that God has shown me how He has been working through me and through so many other people. My premise is that if you have gotten this far in reading this book, then you too are one through whom God has been working and continues to work. My belief is that once you realize this truth, you will have a much more dynamic testimony and witness going forward from here.

Having asserted this premise, I have a very troubling question, which basically remains unanswered. Experts who specialize in doing surveys claim that 85%

of parents with children under age 13 *believe* that they have primary responsibility for teaching their children about religious beliefs. However, the *majority* of those same parents spend NO time each week sharing with these children about their religious beliefs and matters of faith. My question is, "How can this be true and if it is, then where do we go from here and what do we do about this?"

Further data reveal that these children get to Sunday school and church only once or rarely twice a month, yet parents rely on their church to do all the religious training of the children. Having come from a culture and background where, as a child, we had family devotions and Bible reading nearly daily in our home and were required to attend Sunday school and church every Sunday without fail (except for sickness), this data frightens me.

Has our affluence supplied us with second and third homes at the beach or in the mountains, which call to us relentlessly on weekends? Has our appetite for viewing and participating in sports of varying types and levels pulled us out of our church pew? Does our travel out of our area on weekends find us searching out a church to which we can spend one hour in worship? Is God beginning to speak through us and tell us to forget our worship of Him if we are too busy with other things? Friends, we are in dangerous territory. We are "showing" our children and grandchildren that other things are more important to us than our worship of God.

I am sure that we, as grandparents, also need a value check. Perhaps we are the ones supplying our grandchildren with excuses to be out of touch with God through our lifestyles and obvious appearance of self-sufficiency. As I keep saying, "God is working through you and in some cases teaching the grandchildren either right or wrong through our example." God expects our worship and praise. Beyond this, our most important responsibility is to teach our children and grandchildren to respect and worship God. Again I say, it is why we were created.

After retirement and a hiatus away from both administration and the physical location of the ministry at Peter Becker Community and my part-time transition work as a Trust Officer for 5 years, I decided it would be good to consider moving back to campus as a resident. It took some conversation and convincing of my wife Diane, but we finally applied for a duplex cottage. These cottages were totally familiar to me because I had a direct part with the architect in the design and size of them. After a couple calls by the admissions person about a unit coming available, we finally made a decision to make the big move. This was about nine years after retirement (2002) and being totally away from the operation and program per se.

The decision to give up our home, which we had built thirty years before, was much more difficult for Diane than for me. She is a few years younger and had just retired herself with plans in mind to enjoy our home a while longer. She was also aware, however, that I had some health issues and that I was trying to protect her future by joining the active, retired family at PBC and surrounding her with new friends in the event something should happen to me. Now we could both feel secure that any intervening sickness or health concern short of hospitalization would be assured. After the move was consummated, it was interesting for me to now view life as a resident instead of management staff. Not long after moving and resettling in our independent living retirement unit, I again had someone close to me encourage me to write about the history and stories of Peter Becker Community.

CHAPTER 19

This time, the idea occurred to me like a fresh idea—history and stories. I began to ponder the reality that of the persons who originally planned and started the ministry here, only a couple of us remained. All the rest had passed on to the large retirement community in the skies. All of the difficult beginnings would soon fall by the wayside if not written down. I am not a fan of histories. I think most of them, at least the ones I was forced to learn in high school, are boring. Who cares about all those dates and places? As I have aged, I have come to appreciate history more than before. Nevertheless, I considered that if I wrote just plain history of the beginnings of the ministry at PBC, many would not finish reading the book due to disinterest.

Then I considered the stories and a lightbulb turned on in my mind saying that if the stories caused people to laugh and find interesting, then I would try to weave the stories into the history to make the history more interesting. On that premise, I began to write out some of the stories and some of the history to see where I might finally end up. I was amazed at how easily the stories came to me. I even remembered names, for the most part, and that was a miracle, since my retention memory for names has become a large problem for me. The history was mostly written by memory as well, but to be sure, I referred to Board Minutes for confirmation and accuracy. On many occasions I would be sitting at the computer typing away, then suddenly realize that three or four hours had magically disappeared. It became fun, to my surprise.

When I had completed most of the rough draft of the manuscript, I became concerned that I had pictures for almost each historical event such as buildings and people, but I had no pictures of "stories" which I incorporated into the text. While pondering this, it occurred to me that my good friend, Leon Moyer, who is a commercial artist and sign-painter, had a special gift for drawing spontaneous illustrations/cartoons. I challenged him by suggesting he read the manuscript and if during the reading of any story, a picture came to mind, he should sketch it out. I might be able to use the sketches to support and illustrate the story being written. I hoped for half a dozen or so and he surprised me with seventeen illustrations suitable for printing. I was able to ultimately use all of them to make the reading of the book much more interesting.

At this juncture, I contacted a publishing house recommended to me and asked for an interview. I presented my work—written, pictures and sketches—to the publisher along with my desire to have a first class book with hard cover and dustcover. I was a bit anxious, never having presented a work for consideration of publication. Would they laugh and say no thanks? What would I do then?

They gave me some input regarding disclaimer, table of contents and preface on which I was still working. We agreed they would compute costs, approximate time to publish and delivery processes. In summary they said they were interested and even excited about the project and after all corrections were made they could have it published within 6 weeks. I drove back home feeling proud and exhilarated by the experience.

The story has come full circle. The pride and exhilaration I was feeling is the same set of feelings I shared with you in the first paragraph and chapter of this book. It was at this point that God cleared my head and let me know that *He was directing my steps*.

In the intervening chapters I have tried to show how my recollections of my own life's journey showed me, without a doubt, that God had been working through me—even when I was unaware of it and even though I may not have acknowledged it. My obvious hope is that each reader will try to recount their own life journey with an eye to recognizing their walk with God and His using their talents to accomplish His purposes.

We are currently in a society where there is much unrest and from a prophecy standpoint, we are seemingly drawing closer and closer to the end of time when we expect Jesus to return. It is therefore even more important that each of us recognize our responsibility to others to share God's message and to be open

COINCIDENCE OR GOD'S PLAN

conduits through whom He can work. Satan's forces are trying to impede worship of God, remove His name from schools, government and society, in the belief that will stop God. It is a great feeling to realize that every day we hear of God breaking through these efforts of sinful man in a variety of ways. I'd like to share one of these I recently learned about for your inspiration and encouragement.

Forty years ago this past July was the 40th anniversary of man's first walk on the moon. Buzz Aldrin and Neil Armstrong stepped onto the moon surface as millions of us watched. Some persons still feel it was a set in Hollywood producing the images we saw on television. Eric Metaxas, in his book *Everything You Always Wanted to Know About God (But Were Afraid to Ask)* interviewed Buzz Aldrin and also *Guideposts* magazine wrote about the fact that Aldrin took communion on the surface of the moon.

The background of the story is that Aldrin was an elder at his Presbyterian Church in Texas during this period in his life, and knowing that he would soon be doing something unprecedented in human history, he felt he should mark the occasion somehow, and he asked his pastor to help him. And so the pastor consecrated a communion wafer and a small vial of communion wine. Buzz Aldrin took them with him out of the Earth's orbit and on to the surface of the moon. He and Armstrong had only been on the lunar surface for a few minutes when Aldrin made the following public statement: "This is the Lunar Module pilot. I'd like to take this opportunity to ask every person listening in, whoever and wherever they may be, to pause for a moment and contemplate the events of the past few hours and to give thanks in his or her own way." He ended radio communication and there, on the silent surface of the moon, 250,000 miles from home, he read a verse from the Gospel of John, and he took communion. Herewith, in his own words, is his account of what happened:

"In the radio blackout, I opened the little plastic packages which contained the bread and the wine. I poured the wine into the chalice our church had given me. In the one-sixth gravity of the moon, the wine slowly curled and gracefully came up the side of the cup. Then I read the Scripture, 'I am the vine, you are the branches. Whoever abides in me will bring forth much fruit. Apart from me you can do nothing.' I had intended to read my communion passage back to earth, but at the last minute (they) had requested that I not do this. N.A.S.A. was already embroiled in a legal battle with Madelyn Murray O'Hare, the celebrated opponent of religion, over the Apollo 8 crew reading from Genesis while orbiting the moon at Christmastime. I agreed reluctantly.

"I ate the tiny Host and swallowed the wine. I gave thanks for the intelligence and spirit that had brought two young pilots to the Sea of Tranquility. It was interesting for me to think: the very first liquid ever poured on the moon, and the very first food eaten there were communion elements."

And of course, it's interesting to think that some of the first words spoken on the moon were the words of Jesus Christ, who made the Earth and the moon and Who, in the immortal words of Dante, is Himself the "Love that moves the Sun and other stars." WOW!!! Buzz Aldrin was allowing God to speak through him to all of us.

Long before Jesus came to earth and explained scripture and the law to us, a wise fellow by the name of

Solomon wrote in Proverbs 16:9. "In his heart, a man plans his course, but the Lord determines his steps." It's exactly what I've been feeling and trying to say in this book. Many of us go from day-to-day making decisions and living our lives as best as we know how BUT when we review our journey, we realize that it was God, all along who was and is directing our steps.

God created us. None of us is without sin (I John 1:8). We all need to accept Jesus and acknowledge Him as our Savior. He died to save us from Satan's clutches and offer us eternal life.

Our job—accept this stupendous gift. Thank God each day for this gift. Realize that God has been and continues to work through us. Invite Him to continue with our cooperation and continued assistance. Experience a renewed excitement as we feel this happening and as we journey together with Him throughout our lifetimes. You will begin to recognize coincidence as God's Plan in many instances.

God works through people to do His work. He works through US to continue His Plan. Joseph was sold by his brothers as a slave. God's Plan to get a man in Egypt to plan for and handle the famine to come.

COINCIDENCE OR GOD'S PLAN

Pharaoh's daughter finds baby Moses in the bulrushes by the river Nile. Coincidence—No—God's Plan. Esther approaches the King at the risk of death to save the Jewish people. David is chosen "out of the field" to be a King. Phillip goes where God sends him—meets a chariot, reads to the driver from Isaiah 53, baptizes the new believer. Saul is confounded on the road to Damascus.

Ananias is sent by God to minister to Saul. Saul is converted—he becomes Paul, the missionary to the Gentiles and perhaps the most influential Christian ever, writing vast portions of the New Testament. They were all a part of God's Plan and so are you. Be still and listen for the "voice of God." He speaks to us in many ways. God bless your walk.